BOTTOM UP

An Integrated Neurological and Cognitive Behavioural Book
Which Addresses the Key Principles of Neuropsychotherapy.
Five Important Emotional Parts of the Brain with Skills Training.

DIONNE H. SHNIDER

authorHOUSE®

AuthorHouse™
1663 Liberty Drive
Bloomington, IN 47403
www.authorhouse.com
Phone: 1 (800) 839-8640

Published by AuthorHouse 11/07/2018

ISBN: 978-1-5462-6675-4 (sc)
ISBN: 978-1-5462-6697-6 (e)

Library of Congress Control Number: 2018913050

Print information available on the last page.

Contents

Acknowledgements

I am excited about this product and will continue research into their efficacy as well as expand to address more psychologically challenging presentations. I would like to thank Jonathan Wills and Nita Grayson for editing the initial drafts. And a special thank you to my supportive colleagues and dear friends for their input, testimonials and encouragement to complete this book *Dr. Antonette T. Dulay; Dr. April M. Colbert, Nadine Beile, Nicole Gerschman and Rita Princi.*

Special thanks to all the clients, researchers and animators who provided many hours of support to get these products on the professional level that they present.

A word of great thanks to my family and friends for their consistent support.

And in memory of my mentor and close friend who gave so much of himself in sharing his passion of neuroscience fundamentals.

About the Author

Dr. Dionne Shnider is a licensed psychologist and Certified Applied Neuroscience Practitioner in private practice. She has worked as a psychologist within a variety of settings – including mental health, psychology service in courts and occupational and vocational rehabilitation – both in public and private organisations. Dionne's private practice makes extensive use of the metaframework neuropsychotherapy, evidence-based psychological therapies, advanced Cognitive Behavioural Therapy (CBT) and Solution Focused Therapy. She is the author of The Neuroscience Toolkit for Clinicians. She has worked in The Netherlands, United States and Australia. She currently holds the role as advisor for the International Associations of Applied Neuroscience IAAN.

Foreword

It is hoped and intended that this book will fill a gap in existing resources by contributing to the meta-framework that is shaping psychotherapy today. These relate to the prevention of negative behavioural irregularities and the absence of an integrated neurological and cognitive behavioural manual. The manual will aim ultimately to prevent the clinical expression of primary or secondary conditions like generalised anxiety disorder, depression, obsessional compulsive disorders, sleep disturbance and general mood disorders, and to build neural resilience for clients, so their capacity to succumb to future psychological unwellness is strengthened.

This book has six main sections. The first section will be an introduction explaining the key principles of neuropsychotherapy. The rest of the book is divided into five units that are short enough so that you can usually work through each section without interruption. Each section deals with an important emotional part of the brain and introduces a group of skills accompanying it, which may be applied in the relevant circumstances.

Try to avoid taking on too much at once, give yourself time to understand and assimilate what you have learned, before moving onto the next unit. Give your brain a chance to digest and process the information and to build new neural networks!

Explaining the Key Principles of Neuropsychotherapy

Neural Underpinnings

Freud studied widely in the area of human behaviour and he observed extensively the factors which were associated with the responses people made to their environment. His work led to recognising the association of stress with some disturbance in infancy, and developing his therapies focusing on the reconnection of those whole body experiences a baby receives in the interactions with its mother.

Later, he expanded his work to include how the unconscious mind works in the processing of stress and made the association with the biological factors in the workings of the brain. This initial "top-down approach," suggested that therapists should help decompose the big pictures of behaviours until they were able to get down to the basic experiences of the individual, in an effort to isolate the basic experiential segment that had been disrupted. At that point that behaviour would be re-modelled to the individual.

For example, if a person was not cuddled as a child, cuddling would be introduced in therapy in an effort to supply what the person had missed in childhood. Freud recognised that there was something in the brain holding memories of experience which connected with the foundational affective processes that required rebuilding. This suggested to Freud that the biology of the brain must be somehow involved.

It wasn't until 1998, when Eric Kandel (1998) wrote a paper drawing on Freud's and others earlier work, in which he insisted that therapeutic work must not only consider the behaviours of a person, but also the brain's ability to actually rebuild new structures (this was at that time just becoming visible in brain imaging studies).

In other words, Kandel was advocating a neurobiological approach that worked not from the top down but from the bottom up. Therapy should examine the details of brain functioning and processing elements within the client and how receptive information is handled or perceived in an individual's brain.

Allan Schore (2012, p.1) continued with this line of research stating "no theory of human functioning can be restricted to only a description of psychological processes; it must also be consonant with what we now know about biological structural brain development". So, in order to fully understand this concept between the biology of the brain and behavioural coping mechanisms an individual uses under stress, the physical structure of the brain must be understood.

The ideas about understanding the workings of various parts of the brain, and looking into how both brain structure and brain processing inform the theory of neuropsychotherapy and how it's application can help to regulate behavioural responses, began to rapidly take hold.

Neural Communication

The connection between science and health is a direct one, and our ability to understand the science behind health, affects our ability to understand the issues and the risks; science may seem difficult to understand because scientists often use technical language to talk about abstract ideas.

As the study of genetics give us more information about ourselves, that information increasingly plays a major role in the diagnosis and treatment of disease, even mental disease or, more accurately, disorders. These studies correlate to working from the "bottom-up".

The classic "nature vs. nurture" debate is being balanced daily as the research shows that nature (genetics) and nurture (environmental factors and relationships) work together to make us who we are and how we respond to stimuli.

An increasing number of genetic tests are becoming available commercially, although the scientific community continues to debate the best way to deliver them to the public - and some medical communities may be unaware of their scientific and social implications. While some of these tests have greatly improved and even saved lives, scientists remain unsure about how to fully interpret many of them in the context of psychological unwellness.

Most people are curious about the way their bodies work and this curiosity goes beyond immediate concerns about any specific health condition. However, patients taking the tests may face significant risks of jeopardising their employment or insurance status, and because genetic information is shared, these risks can extend beyond them to their family members as well.

The human genome includes a map of how the brain develops those fixed genetic markers and integrates them within a matrix of neurochemical modification of other genes due to the environment or our perception of things happening in the environment. Since the brain is 'switched on' most of our lives, this matrix is complex.

All communication between the neurons is either a chemical or electrical impulse that darts back and forth between neurons. The neurotransmitters that carry these signals vary, as does the rate of their work (The Neuropsychotherapy Institute, 2014a) and both can be attributed to nature and nurture.

Neurochemicals and Neurotransmitters

Knowing about the neurochemicals, whose job is to modulate and activate the nervous system, is a starting point in understanding the cause and effect of intervention therapies and what contributes to their effectiveness.

The Neuropsychotherapy Institute (2014b), explains these five groups of neurochemicals.

Amino Acid Neurotransmitters

There are two types of amino acid neurotransmitters. The first are glutamates, which are mostly excitatory transmitters. They contribute to the brain's plasticity by strengthening the long-lasting bonds between slower acting neurons that are attributed to memory and learning.

The second is gamma-aminobutyric acid (GABA), an inhibitory neurotransmitter. It binds with GABA receptors to cause an inhibiting effect on the postsynaptic cell membrane. This means the presence of GABA prolongs the interaction between neurons which affects thought processes and sensory input/output processing.

Biogenic Amines

These are neurochemicals that sometimes act as neurotransmitters. Again, there are two main types.

Catecholamines trigger physiological transitions in preparation for fight or flight responses, e.g. dopamine is one catecholamine that has several functions including release during reward-motivated behaviour and in motor control. Atypical antipsychotics (AAPs) may contain synthetically produced dopamine, which are prescribed as a mood stabilisers.

The second type of catecholamine is indolamine. These are neurotransmitters that include serotonin and melatonin which play a part in the regulation of mood, appetite, sleep, memory and learning. Serotonin is a major endogenous hormone, which is synthetically manufactured and included in antidepressant selective serotonin reuptake inhibitors (SSRIs).

Acetylcholine is a neurotransmitter that is used by only a few cell groups in the autonomic ganglia. Peptides are a large and diverse neurotransmitter grouping and includes hormones, enkephalins and endorphins. Other neurotransmitters include histamine and epinephrine, along with over 60 others that are not yet identified.

Activation Patterns and Neural Systems

Neurotransmission is a binary function, a neuron is firing or not firing. Neurons respond to each other, and the environment through sensory cells in an organised and hierarchal system. This complex system hosts an average of 10,000 connections that build neural net profiles, each representing one aspect of the various functions of the brain, like perceiving sound and smell. Neurotransmission is a mechanism of the nervous system, located in many parts of the brain, and exhibits specific activation patterns in response to specific stimuli (Grawe, 2007). Grawe's work on this hierarchical model for processing information is based on the work of neurophysiologists David Hubel and Torsten Wiesel (2012).

This organised system, (from sensory input, i.e. what is perceived of complex objects and an understanding of complex cognitive and affective processes), receives the fragmented pieces of data into the brain. These pieces of data or information activate the neurons and contribute to the assembly of the neural networks. The information is processed from the beginning (the reception of data stimuli from outside the body) to reassembling and toward the recognition of a whole "picture" or a concept, in the network of neural cells in the cortex of the brain.

As the brain 'perceives' this broader picture, it further processes in a parallel processing system to other brain regions. In these other regions of the brain there is further interaction within cells integrating stimuli (both in external and internal) into a compete thought or visualisation of an object, feeling, or concept (Siegel, 2012). From this place, the brain begins another aspect of the organisational processing similar to the physical structuring of the central nervous system. It begins to process yet more complex networks that represent specific areas of the cortex with many input features. The processing is interactive and moves in patterns. Specific areas in the cortex then work to increase the brains ability to assimilate this information with other information already stored in the brain.

Paul MacLean, (1990) a neurologist, described the structure and functional components of the human brain as the 'triune brain'. His theories revolutionised brain studies about how information is stored and processed within the brain. MacLean asserted that the brain has three main structures which have developed in an evolutionary hierarchy: the primitive "reptilian" complex (the brainstem), the "paleomammalian" complex (the limbic system), and the "neomammalian" complex (the neocortex) (MacLean, 1990). He describes the primitive "reptilian" complex to be fully developed at birth, the "paleomammalian" complex partly developed but continuing to develop into childhood, and the "neomammalian" complex, very underdeveloped at birth and the last area of the brain to complete development (Rossouw, 2011; The Neuropsychotherapy Institute, 2014c).

This triune brain model asserts that survival instincts develop first with cognitive processing following later in evolution. MacLean uses this as a basis for the "bottom-up" approach to brain study. This "bottom-up" approach used in therapeutic intervention is the opposite of the "top-down" or cognitive approach in therapy. The bottom-up approach seeks to establish an atmosphere of safety first, by a down-regulation of sympathetic over-arousal, and then in an activation of a state of parasympathetic security. When this is achieved, left frontal cortex blood flow is increased and results in effective activation of cognitive abilities. It also results in interrupting loops of negative activity in the limbic system (Rossouw, 2011, p.4). Only when this occurs, can clients become fully engaged in new learning.

Lain McGilchrist, in his book *The Master and His Emissary: The Divided Brain and the Making of the Western World* (2009), described the asymmetry of the brain. He discussed the different features of both lateral sides of the brain (the left and the right). It gave a horizontal interpretation of the mental system that was at variance with the vertical triune perspective. It highlighted the distinctive differences and also the complimentary functions of the two hemispheres of the brain. McGilchrist explains that the right hemisphere handles broad attention or what gains our attention initially, making connections with other parts of the brain to help an individual acknowledge the wholeness of objects and concepts, how they change over time, are in tune with emotions and exhibit empathic, intuitive, and moral thinking. In the left hemisphere, the input is narrow, focuses on the parts of the whole, decomposes each part and is mostly involved in more static processing involving decontextualised, inanimate structures and abstractions.

McGilchrist (2009) continues in his clarification of the two hemispheres noting that the right brain is the area where a person will experience a live, complex, embodied world of unique beings and objects, always changing yet interdependent, always forming and reforming and giving us a feeling of belonging. His description of the left hemisphere is of an experience that is totally different from the right. In the left brain things are separated, bounded, fragmented, but none-the-less grouped, so it allows some ability to make predictions about the information received. This left part of our brain will isolate each step of the information we receive enabling us to understand exactly and explicitly how things work. This helps us learn how things work, why they work, and enables us to figure out how to manipulate information to make things. It gives human beings total power over the information they receive.

Allan Schore (2012) connects the early-maturing right hemisphere with the basics for attachment formation between infants and their caregivers. This formation in the right hemisphere is then connected to the learning of affect regulation later in life. The research shows that this connection between the formation of attachment and affect regulation later in life directs the central focus of most clinical interventions. Badenoch (2008) suggests that therapist who do not ground their therapy in right brain engagement risk a total disconnect with their client. If therapy should begin in the cognitive realm, clinicians would never get past trying to help their client's see the 'reality' (according to the clinician) of the situation in which they find themselves. A therapist has to connect to individuals in therapy through their affect processing right brain (inducing the mirror neurone system) until their clients are able to regulate and integrate their thinking and feeling states into the self-reflective cognitive realm, which takes much longer, assuming this can be achieved at all.

Neural Mechanisms of Approach and Avoidance Learning

The basic needs of a baby for food, comfort, and sleep, develop over time to become the motivational system in the brain that works to meet a person's needs. There are two motivational systems that develop and work totally independent from each other. The neural layers that make up the network and the mechanisms that create each to operate is also separate. They can and do operate at the same time in a parallel manner and because they are equally strong, though they tend to inhibit each other. As a child grows these networks become more sophisticated in the activation to achieve a person's goals as well as to meet his needs. Each system has its own function. One is steered by approach motivations, the need to be closer to something. The other is steered by avoidance motivations, the strive to put as much distance as possible between the person and whatever it is they want to avoid.

The infant's first development is in the approach system. A baby naturally needs to be close to food, care, and comfort. Attachment to the person who provides these grows and soon the motivation to have his needs met are integrated with a motivation to be with this person. Over time the baby learns more and more behaviours that to gain more success or positive feelings. The mother and the baby are rewarded in this relationship to remain close and neural activation patterns form in the brain that represent this and other goals. The production of oxytocin and dopamine that is released when these goals are met adds strength to the behaviours. A very sophisticated neural pattern continues to expand resulting in spontaneously activated schemas. The brain picks up on needs that are similar to other needs until the organization of the patterns gets quite multifaceted. Growth of an individual brings a wider environment, social expectations, limitations, and other forces, cultural and environmental that continually shape and reshape the neural architectures of the neural patterns. Physiologically, approach goals are associated with the left dorsolateral prefrontal cortex (PFC) and with positive emotions. Avoidance patterns are more associated with the right dorsolateral prefrontal cortex and negative emotions.

This neural network that sets about to motivate or evaluate the approach-positive and the avoidance-negative are lateralised across the brain physiologically. Research shows that this lateralization of these two systems is also seen in the deeper limbic system giving credibility to the theory that approach and avoidance systems are neutrally independent. Because the approach system tends to maximise pleasure and the avoidance system minimises pain, it can be seen how closely related these two separate concepts really are. Both systems work to close the gap between goal and need and in the same way. The differences are in how each system defines closing the gap. In the approach motivation, you are literally working to bring the goal and yourself closer. Along the way there are markers that let you know you are making progress and that in itself feels like success.

For example, in losing weight, if your goal is 10 kilos and you lose five, then six, and so on you begin to feel successful even before the goal is reached. In a university course you do not enjoy, the success comes only when the course is completed, often regardless of high grades along the way. The attainment of some goals are more easily noticed than others.

In the avoidance motivation, the goal is to avoid something altogether. Often it is an ongoing process of prevention. A person wants to avoid upsetting their spouse so he has to remain vigilant every day for as long as that remains his goal. His bar for success is not exact and is ongoing without end.

Other avoidance goals will demonstrate a success. Perhaps you want to avoid being the last one in the race. You train and work hard enough, not to necessarily win but to avoid coming in last. The race comes and you come in next to last. Success!

In the search for a goal that is an approachable goal, positive feelings come from just reaching benchmarks along the way. In the move to avoid something, there is less positive reward and more negative. There is less satisfaction as well due to the amount of disproportionate energy and focus it takes to avoid anything. Investing in strongly developed avoidance behaviours, either implied or specific have unfavorable effects on a person's mental health, feelings of self-worth and well-being. (Grawe, 2007).

In psychotherapy, from the perspective of neuropsychotherapy, avoidance goals should be reduced and approach goals increased in the satisfaction of needs. Depression is often seen in hyper-activation of avoidance schemas. When this happens, it inhibits the approach schemas and the negative impact of stress hormones can physically damage the hippocampus and deactivate the anterior cingulate cortex. A therapist must focus on turning this around. Gradually reactivating the approach system will regenerate activity in the anterior cingulate cortex and develop stronger prefrontal cortex connections with a result of a positive change for the client.

The Social Brain

In 2014, Cozolino used the term "social brain" to reflect neural systems that form and function within the scope of interpersonal relationships. Interpersonal relationships are defined by the individuals, families, communities, and the norms, mores and cultures that surround us. They shape the way we behave and function in our societies, hopefully nurturing us in those relationships and setting up the patterns in our neural systems which function to maintain those interpersonal relationships. According to Siegel (2012), the middle prefrontal region of the brain includes the insula, orbitofrontal cortex, ventromedial prefrontal cortex, and the anterior cingulate cortex, and the brain convoluted and wraps itself around in each part of this area. It is within this region that integration, planning, and thought processing parts of the cortex and limbic system are interfaced. According to Badenoch (2008), the ventral vagal interaction with the middle prefrontal region, constitutes the neurophysiology of the social system. It regulates communication, flexible responsiveness, affect regulation, empathy, insight, morality, and intuition. When the limbic system exhibits more strength in this integration with the middle prefrontal region, it can influence our emotional experiences. Those strong emotional patterns of experience establish connections between our memory systems and external environmental cues. If an individual is ruminating on past experiences (experiencing negative thoughts and feelings), brain activation between the emotional centre, our anterior cingulate gyrus and survival areas of the brain (brain stem) may continue to form neural loops, partly because our emotional responses to these negative thoughts and feelings are self-reinforcing. If the middle prefrontal region (regulating affect, insight and responsiveness) can become stronger than the limbic system activation, through repeated neural activation (prompted by neuropsychotherapeutic interventions), the middle prefrontal region will be developed such that it may more readily regulate our emotional responses.

The most primitive functions of the social brain are based in the affectively and somatically biased right hemisphere. This is where the "bottom-up" processing of emotional and social information dominates (Schore, 2012; Cozolino, 2014). If left and right hemispheres of the brain are integrated in a balanced way, and cortical and subcortical systems are well developed and integrated, an individual is likely to find more success in their social world.

Clinical Application of Neuropsychotherapy

The clinical application of neuropsychotherapy focuses on strengthening clients' resources from the core of their motivational systems, to facilitate an increasingly robust approach of *self* and a persons' place in the world (Flückinger, Wüsten, Zinbarg, & Wampold, 2009). When this can be achieved, a client is more likely to find greater satisfaction in meeting their basic needs and in their own mental well-being. For the clinical application of neuropsychotherapy to work effectively, a "safe" therapeutic alliance must be facilitated within an approach pattern that will satisfy basic needs and down-regulate stress activation. New optimal and positive neural connections must then be reinforced with those that already exist.

Controllable Incongruence as the Lever for Change

When a person's perception of reality significantly diverges from what that person believes and expects in any given situation, and also when the goals they set are not realised, it may result in such strong feelings of *uncontrollable* incongruence that an inconsistency is developed within the function of the mental system (Grawe, 2007). In a clinical situation, it is *controllable* incongruence that becomes the mechanism of change in the therapeutic dyad (between the therapist and their client). What we are aiming to achieve in therapy is for the client to experience controlled incongruence, so that the client feels they are able to cope with such a challenge. If we work too quickly and force change when the client is not ready, this may result our client experiencing uncontrollable incongruence, which usually exceeds an individual's ability to cope, or may even alter their belief that they can cope. In this circumstance, there is such a discordant state between what a client experiences and any goals which are set, the experience of their psychological unwellness may become overwhelming. They may experience stress that heightens arousal, potentially beyond their tolerance level. If this situation is not resolved it can result in a hyperactivated hypothalamus, pituitary, adrenal (HPA)-axis cascade, releasing damaging amounts of glucocorticoids into the bloodstream and bodily systems. Glucocorticoids can reduce inflammation and calm immune cells, but in excess and for prolonged periods they also have negative effects and can lead to weight gain, weakened bones, diabetes, high blood pressure, thin skin, slow healing, acne, fatigue, depression and other damaging conditions.

If the stress response is regulated, a feedback loop will down-regulate the HPA-axis activation and force the release of parasympathetic hormones (Kandel, Schwartz, Jessell, Siegelbaum, & Hudspeth, 2013). If the stress response is allowed to continue, the ongoing release of glucocorticoids can inhibit the formation of new synapses (and thus new learning) while at the same time degenerating existing glutamate synapses. It will also effect the healthy function of the hippocampus, destabilising previously formed neural connections or established learning. Prolonged stress responses can even induce complex negative structural changes in various brain regions

(Lupien, McEwen, Gunnar, & Heim, 2009). So, the stress response, (when activated in the absence of a real threat to survival) requires the development for the client of a sense of control that can begin to reduce the cascade of hormonal release and restore HPA-axis regulation.

Controllable incongruence occurs when a specific stressor is raising arousal levels (through sympathetic excitation and noradrenergic activation) and may exceed a given threshold of activation of the HPA-axis, but the situation is perceived as manageable by the client. When it is controlled and internal feedback results in a down-regulation, the stress response remains within normal parameters. In situations of controlled stress a moderate amount of adrenalin enters the nervous system and promotes positive activation of neurons, glia and endothelial cells, facilitating a constructive response (neural connections) to incongruence in the form of learning. This is the exact opposite of what occurs in situations experienced as uncontrolled incongruence. When stress is controlled, even mildly, adrenergic receptors are stimulated within blood vessels and astrocytes, glucose is released increasingly, along with an increase in metabolism. These processes work together in conjunction with the release of neurotrophic factors from astrocytes (Verkhratsky & Butt, 2007). The adrenergic receptors are stimulated and neural connections are activated as the client begins using a successful coping strategy, which improves the path toward creating new neural connections. Through the use of new coping strategies, new and positive neural reinforcement begins. New learning requires the interruption of the negative neural looping, to enable the formation of "…ever more complex and differentiated neural circuits, to an optimal expression of the person's genetic potential." (Grawe, 2007, p. 222).

With continued therapeutic work to establish new coping behaviours and more control over incongruent experiences, eventually such situations will no longer elicit a problematic stress response for the client and new neural networks become established to assess and cope with stress more effectively in the future. So, in therapy the goal is to strengthen existing coping skills and facilitate new coping skills on a neurobiological level, thereby raising overall resilience. This can only happen at the neural level. In the safety of a strong therapeutic alliance, stress responses may be down-regulated to a level which supports learning. Incongruence may be broken down into manageable experiences and controlled with new strategies. Grawe (2007) stresses that motivational priming and resource activation are key elements for controlling incongruence in the learning phase. In a therapeutic session, it is necessary to focus on positive need-satisfying experiences that fit with the client's goals. In the beginning these begin small and specific and provide positive satisfaction of control, attachment, pain avoidance, or self-esteem.

Establishing an effective therapeutic alliance is an example of a positive activation of a need for attachment that would prime the client toward approach-orientated behaviours. When the therapist identifies existing resources, characteristics and abilities the client already has, and the client can see how these are readily achievable and provide support, it is called resource activation. By enhancing these during a session it can enhance the client's feelings of control and self-value and thereby increase tolerance for some short term elevated level of incongruence during the therapy session (Smith & Grawe, 2003). This focus on the client's healthy psychological attributes, lays a foundation for trust. A client often comes to therapy feeling hopeless, and thinking they have no resources within themselves to resolve problems. Before therapeutic change can take place, safety in the therapeutic environment is required and *then* the rebuilding of the client's awareness of his own resources may proceed. Only in this way can a problem activation approach be introduced and be effective in helping the client to change (Gassmann & Grawe, 2006). It is the job of a therapist to work with the client to reactivate their experience of self-effectiveness. A counsellor or therapist ought to be able to highlight the existing strengths and abilities of the client, and lead them toward an experience with which they are able to cope, no matter how small (Flückinger, Wüsten, Zinbarg, & Wampold, 2009, p.2).

Taking advantage of controllable incongruence as a mechanism of change (whilst downregulating from a destructive uncontrolled stress response) will reduce the incongruence between what the client believes they can cope with and immediacy of a client's responses. Once a therapist has been able to gain the trust of the client, the client in likely to be more willing to engage in learning a minimal controlled response to stress. When this happens, the client is allowing the brain's natural neuroplasticity to begin the process of new neural patterning (learning). To establish such a safe environment requires a downregulation of avoidance motivational schemas, that may be activated for the client, and research shows that within the boundaries of the "safe area" and in the therapeutic dyad, an enhanced attachment, control and stress reduction can be effectively facilitated. As this is happening, the client will find that they can begin to increase social interactions that are an essential element of healthy neural proliferation (Allison & Rossouw, 2013, p.23).

This "bottom-up" approach of working with physiological stress responses, before the facilitation of effective neural change and proliferation, is the only way to effectively bring change and control over uncontrollable incongruence experienced by a client. It's dealing with the 'parts of the problems' to reach the whole of the problem. By reconstructing the strengths of the client (and facilitating the client's brain processing), acquired and learned through trust in the therapeutic alliance and the client's mirroring of the counselor's right brain approach in therapy, the uncontrolled stress responses are minimised (Allison & Rossouw, 2013; Rossouw, 2012b, 2012c, 2013b).

In above-mentioned activity, the therapist connects with the client to downregulate the limbic system whilst taking advantage of "mirror neurone" activity. This is accomplished by communicating an empathic, supportive relationship that satisfies the basic need for attachment (Schore, 2012) and happens in a safe therapeutic relationship. Facilitating neural proliferation is integrated within the therapy because the nervous system is essentially a 'social-centric system' that thrives on interpersonal love, acceptance, and security (Cozolino, 2014; Schore, 2012; Siegel, 2012). This takes us back to the earlier mentioned decreased blood flow in the left PFC, which contributes to anxious affect and to increased blood flow in the right PFC, which inhibits the ability of the left PFC to modulate emotional arousal. When the left PFC is engaged and activated in a safe therapeutic environment, more blood flows to it, allowing for modulation of the right cortical and limbic areas (The Neuropsychotherapy Institute,

2014d). The body (sympathetic nervous system responses) will actually take certain areas of the brain "offline" to provide increased blood supply for more essential areas such as the right PFC and limbic areas in times of threat or danger (just as the body will slow the function of certain organs to allow the function of critical organs when a body starved, or during other physiological stresses) (The Neuropsychotherapy Institute, 2014d). When this "offline" system is needed to downregulate an overreaction, (one elicited by a hyperactive amygdala) the feeling of uncontrollable incongruence increases.

In order to mitigate the problem of an essential control system (like the PFC) shutting down in times of stress, there must be an increase in integrative connectivity to areas in the brain that use higher-order control. When such integration is achieved, the learned downregulation of emotional systems and greater activation of the PFC has a greater controlling influence on the brain, and so is less likely to get shut down. Mindfulness is a practice that can achieve this. Mindfulness focusses our attention on the present, without judgement (Kabat-Zinn, 1994, 2013). It can increase mid-PFC and right anterior insula activity and thickening, increasing activity in the superior temporal gyrus and anterior cingulate (Badenoch, 2008). The practice of mindfulness will increase the integration of these systems with the limbic system and result in in better modulatory control over amygdala overreactions. Mindfulness fosters a propensity to approach rather than avoid challenging situations (Siegel, 2012), bringing overwhelming situations back into the realm of controllable incongruence. Research on this has continually shown that meditative practices like mindfulness not only increase the integration and plasticity of neural networks, but may also slow aging processes and increase our ability to be presently attuned and compassionate toward others (Badenoch, 2008).

Siegel (2007) suggests that changing our language, especially during self-talk, will gain greater prefrontal management of limbic responsiveness. By using a different kind of language to express feelings and to move from negative feelings to a more objective and observable phenomenon that is "beyond the self", gives a person a greater sense of control, (as opposed to an immersive emotional experience). An example of this is when, you may say to yourself, "I'm just so sad and depressed." To put the emotions this self-talk elicits (i.e. sadness, depressed affect) 'outside' of yourself, to see it as something outside of your body, helps separate the emotion from 'self', so that you can "observe your 'self'." To achieve this through self-talk we must change the language to "There is something around that is sad and depressing." The research on this process indicates that a person may elicit a greater sense of control over the feeling when it is re-expressed in objective form, rather than allow the negative thought to take control. Using a mindfulness strategy has several positive outcomes. There is less dysregulation and reactivity to emotional experiences; it keeps an individual within thoughts and feelings in the present (avoiding rumination or regrets about the past and worry or concern about the future); avoids moving toward negative feelings that creep in; allows for thoughts or actions without distraction; gives a person the ability to label the negative feeling; to consider a person's own beliefs, opinions and expectations about their thoughts and feelings; and all with a nonjudgmental stance toward the personal experience that is taking place (Badenoch, 2008; Baer, Smith, Hopkins, Krietemeyer, & Toney, 2006).

Motivational priming, resource activation, creating safety, and techniques like mindfulness are all designed to bring the client into a place of optimal learning. In this place, incongruence is perceived as tolerable and controllable and allows the opportunity for new learning and positive change, both in the outward life of that person and inside his brain.

Guide to using the book

This guide will give support and direction for using this book. Using this guide, you will have a set of images, diagrams, worksheets, and supporting research and explanations of key principals in understanding neurobiology and the cause and effect of effective intervention therapies for the "bottom-up" therapeutic method to be successfully implemented.

This book is founded on what's called the "bottom-up" approach. It requires building trust in the therapeutic alliance, down regulating anxious and fearful affect, identifying strengths, identifying and increasing insight into learned responses, and an understanding of the brain and its processes, with a right and left brain method in each session. The book is designed to be tailored to the unique experience of your needs, and you will be able to select the appropriate tools to accommodate this.

This book is comprised of five separate sections, each focused on one condition (set of symptoms) that affects mental health: general anxiety disorder, panic disorder, depression, obsessive compulsive disorder, and sleep disorders.

Each section uses illustrations, worksheets and suggestions for journaling to address each mental health issue.

Included in the book:

- A foreword about the book which provides background on neuropsychotherapy to reinforce the processes for behavioural change, learning and understanding from a research perspective (with references).
- Guide to using the book, encouraging your brain to recover from survival mode, to thrive and learn.

- Worksheets and exercises specific for each presenting problem and for ease of individualising processes toward emotional self-control.
- Addition articles and information which support the worksheets and illustrations, integrate neurobiological and cognitive behavioural theories, incorporate key principles of neuropsychotherapy, and provide suggestions about managing each condition.

The book is unique in its approach because it provides an integrated neurobiological and cognitive behavioural approach that incorporates the key principles of neuropsychotherapy. Currently, it supports five separate presenting problems and related brain activity, along with specific skills training. The book gives an easy and individualised process toward greater emotional self-control for you.

Guidance and direction

Step 1: Become familiar with the book to allow a better grasp of the content. It provides the ability to focus on one presenting problem or more than one.

- Look through the worksheets and exercises specific for each presenting problem.

Step 2: Review the specific details and instructions for each unit. Unpack the content so you become familiar with the whole process and to allow a better grasp of the content.

- Examine the realities of the presenting problem and how it affects you personally, referring to the information in the written material.
- The connection between science and health is a direct one, and the ability to understand the science behind health, affects a person's ability to understand the issues involved.
- This "bottom-up" approach recognises the concept that survival instincts develop first and then cognitive processing.
- NOTE: The initial "top-down" approach (originally developed by Freud), suggested that the therapist help the client to decompose the big picture of their behaviours until they cognitively

understand their current problems (based on early life experiences and development) in an effort to isolate the basic cognitions or development which had been disrupted.

- Express feelings, thoughts, and work through journaling, worksheets, and skill development.
- From the neuropsychotherapeutic perspective, avoidance goals should be reduced and approach goals increased toward the satisfaction of needs.
- When a person's perception and recognition of reality is separated from what that person believes or expects, and their goals are not met, it results in incongruency and inconsistency in mental functioning.
- Keeping a journal, noting behaviors, thoughts, perceptions, and reflecting on how these compare with personal goals, beliefs and values (which need to be expressed in the journal) will integrate this process with neuro-education.

Step 3: Begin new skills learning by working through the information, worksheets from the toolkit that match the presenting problem, and implementation of journaling.

- This book will help you understand how the brain responds to thoughts, actions, and our social and psychical environment and become aware of personal responses to stress and patterns of brain functioning.
- The book will help you examine how to control your own reactions and downregulate brain hyperactivity, to change a negative response to a positive response and to identify and move away from perceived threatening situations.
- The book will guide you to develop strategies to manage responses and control the escalation of anxious affect. Each strategy is something new that you introduce to put "thinking" and self-control back into brain processing.
- Spend enough time and reflection on each skill before moving to the next, giving your brain time to absorb and make sense of the information and how it can individually be applied.

Step 4: Consistently review the information about brain processing, brain chemicals, and brain refocusing.

- Remember it is a process to break old brain patterns and take control with the new techniques and strategies and building new neural networks.
- New learning and new strategies for ending an escalating response (anxious affect) to imaginary conditions (distortion of reality) requires practice on a regular basis for the brain to change, but it will change.

Final Reminders

Good patterns of sleep, nutrition, exercise and socialising with others will help to maintain healthy levels of brain chemicals and reinforce strong communication and integration between the emotional and the smart brain.

Sometimes medication may help, but this is most effective when you build new brain pathways and develop healthy lifestyle habits.

Changing the brain is not always easy, but it's worth the effort to move from un-wellness to thriving and finding more joy in life and a greater level of wellbeing.

Using this guide, you will have a set of images, diagrams, supporting research and explanations of key principles for understanding neurobiology and the cause and effect of successful intervention therapies that use the "bottom up" therapeutic approach.

Understand how the brain develops from the bottom up

How the brain develops

This is Steve like us Steve has three key parts of the brain, that are affected by anxiety.

The first is an area where all the information we receive from the outside world arrives through what we see, hear and feel. We will call this the ignition switch. Once alerted the ignition switch then activates the second part of the brain, the impulsive brain which helps to keep us safe.

 1 Ignition switch

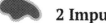 **2 Impulsive brain**

3 Smart brain

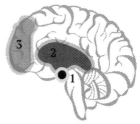

People with high anxiety tend to experience a quick response when the impulsive brain is activated. The third part of the brain affected by anxiety is called the smart brain and it is this part that can help us to control anxiety.

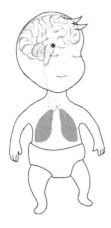

The ignition switch is fully developed when we are born, it tells the heart to pump and the lungs to breathe even when we are asleep.

It is the starting point for responses that may trigger anxiety. Steve's impulsive brain is ready to work at birth too, but it is what happens to him, particularly when he is young that programs this part of his brain.

Steve's ignition switch is set-off when he hears a dog barking nearby, as it approaches him, his impulsive brain is activated by the potential threat. When the dog jumps up to lick him and knocks Steve over, his mother panics and shoves it away.

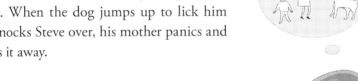

However, Steve's impulsive brain has been activated even further by observing his mother's alarm response to the dog.

Steve's impulsive brain has now been programmed to become active when he encounters any type of dog. The impulsive brain protects us when things are perceived to be dangerous by releasing protective brain chemicals and creating effective patterns of communication in the brain, but sometimes even when there is no real danger, the impulsive brain generalizes and becomes overactive and we are anxious.

The smart brain develops a lot when we are three years old. It can tell the impulsive brain when things are really dangerous or not, using reason and logic. When there is good communication from the smart brain to the impulsive brain, we are no longer anxious.

On seeing his friend approaching with a new puppy, Steve's impulsive brain becomes active again due to his bad experience with the dog.

But when he uses his smart brain to tell him this puppy is friendly, he is able to relax and enjoy giving it a pat.

The more Steve uses his smart brain to tell his impulsive brain to relax, the stronger the smart brain becomes. Steve can enjoy life so much more as he can control his impulsive brain.

Worksheets- How the brain develops

TASK 1

1A. List the three key areas of the brain that are affected by anxiety

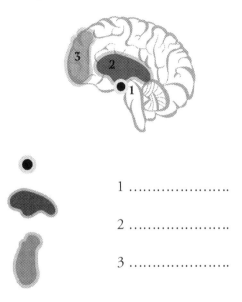

1 ....

2 ....

3 ....

1B. In the table below, identify which explanation matches the areas of the brain 1, 2 or 3 (illustrated above). You can use arrows or rewrite it in your own words.

EXPLANATION	BRAIN AREA
This is an area where all the information we receive from the outside world arrives through what we see, hear and feel. We will call this the ignition switch.	IMPULSIVE BRAIN
The part of the brain which helps to keep us safe.	SMART BRAIN
The part of the brain that can help us to control anxiety.	IGNITION SWITCH

TASK 2

You will need a notebook to use as your *brain journal* throughout this manual. It can be any size or colour you like. Each time you feel unsettled or experience negative emotions, thoughts or feelings, take out your journal and describe what has happened. Here is an example of what to include:

1. The time and place where you were, and when you became anxious
2. What made you anxious, what were you feeling and thinking
3. What you did when you became anxious
4. The consequence of your anxious behaviour

You may wish to write it in a table format, like this:

The time and place where you were, and when you became anxious	What made you anxious, what were you feeling and thinking	What you did when you became anxious	The consequence of your anxious behaviour

TASK 3

Let's start using the journal to identify the things that maintain your anxiety and stress. This involves the way you think, feel and currently cope, that may keep your anxiety and/or feelings of panic going. For the purpose of this exercise we will focus on eight main causes:

1. Avoidance of anxiety provoking situations: It is sometimes easier to avoid situations that may cause us stress rather than actually confronting and dealing with them.
2. Anxious self-talk: This is what you say to yourself in your own mind, which is unhelpful.

3. Inaccurate beliefs: Your internal negative self-talk may stem from inaccurate or irrational beliefs about yourself, others, or external events.

4. Withheld feelings: Not being able to or having the opportunity to express your feelings about sadness, anger, frustration or even happiness, can contribute to feelings of anxiety.

5. Building self-nurturing skills: Gaining greater awareness of your emotional needs and being able to care for yourself emotionally.

6. Muscle tension: When your muscles are tight you automatically feel uptight or on edge. For example, stiff muscles around neck, shoulders and back.

7. Too many stimulants and other dietary factors: Stimulants like nicotine, caffeine and alcohol can aggravate anxiety and leave you more vulnerable to panic attacks. Cutting back on these stimulants and increasing healthy foods, which provide good nutrition, help your body cope with stress and lessen anxiety.

8. Lack of meaning or sense of purpose: Feeling that your life does not have any direction, purpose or meaning.

Look at the list below and identify which of these factors may be maintaining your *feelings* of anxiety?

Try to rank these factors by numbering from 1-8 (according to the highest impact 8, and the lowest impact being 1).

RANK 1-8	FACTOR
	Avoidance of anxiety provoking situations
	Anxious or negative self-talk
	Mistaken beliefs
	Withheld feelings
	Lack of self-nurturing skills
	Muscle tension
	Stimulants
	Lack of meaning or sense of purpose

From the list on page 6, which ones do you feel are most important to work on and why? Are there other feelings you can add that may be missing?

_____

_____

_____

_____

_____

_____

_____

_____

_____

_____

_____

_____

_____

_____

_____

_____

_____

The more insight you have into your thoughts, feelings and behaviour, the more control you will be able to have. Below is a suggestion box of other behaviours.

Suggestion Box

Doing things to get people's attention	Making mistakes
Acting irritably towards others	Skipping meals
Seeking reassurance from others	Acting aggressively towards others
Binge eating	Crying
Putting off doing things	Staying in bed
Following rituals or routines	Self-harming

TASK 4

The "stress response on the brain" -- What does this mean for you?

Write in your journal or communicate to someone what your ***mind*** does when you are stressed? Think about your stress response under the following five categories.

There are no right or wrong responses, describe what stress does to your:

1. Thoughts
2. Emotions
3. Behaviour – to self and/or others
4. Energy levels
5. Avoiding interaction or approaching others

Reflection

Taking a moment to reflect assists us to identify what we need and what we must do to help ourselves. It also helps us identify our strengths and weaknesses and reinforce learned behaviors.

1. Reflect on your learning, thinking and work today. What were you most satisfied about and why?
2. Where did you feel more challenged today, and what did you do to deal with it?
3. What can you do now to steer the road ahead with the most success?

Summary

You should now have greater skills to identify the warning signs your mind and body send you when you are stressed or feeling anxious. When you experience one of your anxious signs, identify your emotions, thoughts and bodily feelings associated with it.

Panic and the brain

Every day we are faced with all sorts of decisions. Like Steve who is now faced with an obstacle - an open man-whole in his path.

Steve's ignition switch is alerted by this potential danger, which in turn sets off his impulsive brain. When in danger the impulsive brain wants us to pay attention and make sure we remain safe.

However Steve's smart brain tells him he doesn't have to run away or fall down this man-whole, he can walk around it.

As simple as this is, Steve has been able to get his impulsive brain and his smart brain to work together to make a good decision. Let us consider how this operates in the brain when we feel anxious. People who experience anxiety find that their impulsive brains get triggered even when there is little or no threat.

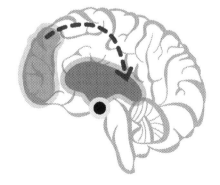

Maybe you had a bad experience with a dog like Steve? Whenever he sees a dog now, Steve wants to run away and gets very panicky. What is happening in his impulsive brain?

The impulsive brain wants to protect us from danger, but when it operates by itself it can get trapped in a vicious counter-productive cycle (loops), which keeps us stuck in our anxiety. The impulsive brain will act like we are in danger, even when we are not.

This causes Steve to breathe more rapidly and his heart to beat faster and he starts to feel 'out of control'. How can Steve assist his brain to change all of this? It is different for each of us but there are several useful activities we can do to help change our brains.

These activities can break damaging loops in the impulsive brain and instead promote strong communication with the smart brain. A good example of this is regular exercise. When we exercise we increase our blood flow to the smart brain, which allows the entire brain to work better.

Writing also activates our blood flow to the smart brain as does talking to someone or when noting to our problems or simply socialising. Eating healthy food also nourishes our bodies with the chemicals our brains need to become more active.

All these things can help us to develop a lifestyle that changes our brain permanently and helps us to manage our lives more effectively - allowing us to breathe easy and relax. Remember

though that this isn't a magic cure. We need to do these activities on a regular basis for the brain to change, but it will change.

Worksheets - Panic and the brain

TASK 1

Reading the signs

It is important to recognise your signs of anxiety and to read them correctly. Some signs are easy to read, like flashing red lights at a railway crossing. Other signs are more subtle like a petrol gage on a car's dashboard. But you have to learn how to read them and to understand their meaning, before we can act on them. This next worksheet is to encourage you to think about what physical and behavioural signs your body sends to alert you that your stress levels are climbing.

We are going to identify your warning signs by documenting how your body feels when you are calm and how it feels when you are anxious.

Start by sitting down somewhere comfortable and where you feel safe. Close your eyes and focus on how your body feels sitting or lying in your chosen space.

Below are two tables – the first table is based on being aware of the physical sensations when you are anxious and the second is for when you are calm and relaxed.

Fill out this table for what your body feels like when it is anxious

Suggestion: Close your eyes and think of an event or time when you felt anxious

ITEM	HOW YOUR BODY FELT (examples)
Body position	*Slouched at kitchen table*
Neck	*Slight soreness on neck strained*
Shoulders	*Up high and tense*
Jaw	*Clenched*

Eyes	*Squinting*
Mouth	*None*
Arms	*Folded in front*
Hands	*Tightly clenched*
Legs	*Tense*
Feet	*Sore pressed hard against floor*
Other	*None*

Fill out this table for what your body feels like when relaxed and calm

Suggestion: Close your eyes and think of an event or time when you calm and relaxed

ITEM	HOW YOUR BODY FELT
Body position	
Neck	
Shoulders	
Jaw	
Eyes	
Mouth	
Arms	
Hands	
Legs	
Feet	
Other	

TASK 2

Identify, Evaluate and Strategy

Of the following three steps, you are well aware of the first one. The second is easy to learn and takes only one of these worksheets. Step three we will introduce a few different coping techniques from which you can select the ones that best suit you.

The three steps are:

1. Identify when you are anxious: You learnt how to do this is the last section. Identifying the physical sensations of your body parts when under stress and feeling anxious.
2. Evaluate the situation: Are you in an unsafe environment or in danger? Usually you are not, but if yes, remove yourself from any danger. If no, you know you are dealing with anxiety or heightened levels of stress.
3. Set up a strategy to manage the anxiety so it does not escalate. A helpful strategy is something that you are probably not doing now. The purpose of the strategy is to put your thinking brain back in charge.

In step 1 you identified your physical and behavioural signs to recognise an emotion that you feel when anxious or stressed. The next step is to determine which emotion you are feeling and why.

This is something you do automatically without a lot of thought. For example, if you are sitting in class and unexpectedly your teacher calls out your name, you recognise the emotion (fear or surprise) and identify the threat (the teacher confronting you) almost without thinking. So, step 2 can be summarised with one question "What is the threat?"

<u>Surprise</u>: If there is no threat at all your mind and body will only feel surprise. You may feel a small amount of adrenalin, and you may experience mild feelings of anxiety, but you can identify straight away that nothing is threatening.

<u>Fear</u>: If there is a physical threat to your health or survival you are feeling fear. You may also be feeling anxiety at the same time. In the first instance, (if you are able to) you will put the anxiety aside and deal with the physical threat. Thought stopping is a positive way of being able to focus on the threat at hand. Force yourself to see an image in your mind to stop the thought, for example, *a stop sign, a red light or the word STOP (review Task 3)*.

<u>Anxiety / panic</u>: Once you have identified and dealt with the fear or threat, whatever is left over is the anxiety / panic. At this point we need to introduce; relaxation techniques (guided breathing and guided meditation), thought stopping and positive self-talk, and time-out techniques (see Table 2, below).

Surprise = no threat = no action

Fear = physical threat = action immediately

Panic/ anxiety = implement techniques
that work for you in the moment

Think of a recent event when you felt surprised, fearful or panicky. Write in the column on the right actions you feel you should have taken

Table 1

EVENT	ACTIONS I FEEL I SHOULD HAVE TAKEN
1. Briefly describe the event	
2. Was there any threat? Yes or No	
3. If you answered Yes to question 2, was there a physical threat to your survival and /or health? Describe it.	
4. If you answered NO to question 2 what was your emotion? Surprise? Fear? Panic?	
5. If there was panic, how did you manage it? Or could you have managed it better?	

TASK 3

Time-out techniques

3A. This technique allows you to become mindful and present in the here and now. This will be done using relaxation imagery. You are going to close your eyes and imagine a peaceful, calm and safe setting for you. The image could be a warm beach, a cosy fireplace with a large comfortable couch, a forest with a slow flowing river, etc.

Sit in a comfortable place where you feel relaxed and safe. You may close your eyes or have them open, whatever feels comfortable for you. Be mindful of how your body feels in this very relaxed and comfortable state. Focus on your chosen imagery and bring all the five senses into mind. Take your time and experience each one. When you are finished, in Table 2, write down your reactions and impressions of each one.

Table 2

SENSE	EFFECT
Sight	
Hearing	
Smell	
Touch	
Taste	

Thought stopping and making it positive

3B. Thought stopping is important in the way of interrupting the negative thoughts that can lead to panic. Whenever you have negative thoughts or feelings of panic, force yourself to try one of the following 3 techniques:

You can stop negative thoughts by doing a few mental time-out techniques. Something as simple as counting backwards in 3's from 100 (100, 97, 94,

91 etc.). Others might include singing a song to yourself or reciting the alphabet backwards. It also provides you time to emotionally regulate and get some good blood flow to your 'smart' brain. Another technique to use is selecting an image that has meaning for you.

For example:

A stop sign   A red Light

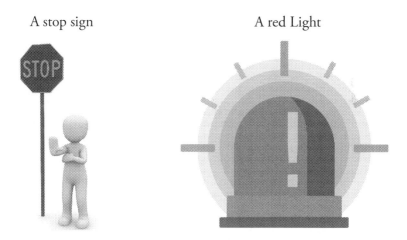

The word **STOP** or **NO**

If mental time-outs are not working for you why not try a physical time-out. It is an action that physically removes you from an anxiety provoking situation. Sometimes just shutting your eyes is sufficient. Or alternatively, going for a walk, run, pushups or squats, listening to music, pod-cast or reading.

Time out techniques are effective ways to interrupt the panic and negative thought cycles. They reinforce that you are in control and they give you time to think of your choices to manage.

TASK 4

In your journal, list a least five time-out techniques that you think you could use in a situation in which your anxiety may escalate to panic, or be initially triggered. Practice makes us feel confident and in control. You will need to test out a few of the techniques to see which one suits the situation at any given time.

Reflection

1. What is the most effective thing you learned today? And what value could that have for your ongoing management?
2. Is there anything you would like to learn more about, and how it can help you moving forward?

Summary

Select the best parts of these four tasks and use them ongoing in your life. Remember the three steps: 1. Recognise your panic, 2. Identify the threat and 3. Use a time out technique to re-gain control.

Depression and the brain

Everyone feels a bit down from time to time. This is a natural part of life, but sometimes people experience low moods more frequently or for longer periods. This is when depression starts to set in and when the general sense of unhappiness can take over your life. There are several factors that can cause depression.

One factor may be low levels of the chemical serotonin a neurotransmitter and one of the 'juices' in the brain. This is what enables information to be sent from the impulsive brain to the smart brain.

Unhelpful neuron wiring in the brain can also lead to our experience of depression. If neurons can't connect and communicate properly we will find that unhelpful thought patterns and feelings start to develop and our brain gets trapped into activation patterns that keep us feeling depressed.

Another factor is our environment. For example, our past experiences, the people around us, our childhood and what happens to us on daily basis. Traumatic life events such as serious accidents, losing a job or a death of a loved one, can seriously affect our mood.

Genetics is another factor that can also play a part. Being diagnosed with depression does tend to run in families. However, this doesn't mean someone who has a family history of depression, will definitely experience depression. A combination of low serotonin levels and poor neuron wiring means there isn't a lot of healthy communication going on between the impulsive brain and the smart brain. This is when our thoughts may get stuck in unhelpful loops in the impulsive brain - much like when we experience anxiety.

However, it is the lack of serotonin that causes the dip in our mood. This affects our thoughts, feelings and behaviours. The most noticeable symptom of depression is the level of disengagement people experience. They become trapped, with no help or rational thinking from their smart brains, and they start to disconnect from the outside world and their everyday experiences may diverge significantly from the experience of others around them.

People with depression tend to stop engaging in fun activities. They go out less often, find it harder to socialise and even to do simple daily tasks. This creates behaviour patterns and of isolation and avoidance, which is slowly reinforced by the unhealthy neuron loops.

If this continues for a long time the brain becomes wired to be depressed. People become used to the state of avoidance and even feel safe with it, even though they know it isn't helpful.

To treat depression, we have to address the lack of serotonin, the faulty neuron-wiring and the unhelpful thoughts loops so we can shift out of those avoidance behavior patterns. We need to engage with the world again and start talking to people and pursuing hobbies or interests. Even just going for a walk will help us get 'out of our heads' and into the world around us for a while. We can also adopt healthy sleeping habits, which will also help a lot.

All of these activities will increase our serotonin levels which will in turn shift the unhelpful neuron wiring, breaking out of unhelpful loops and help link up our impulsive brain with our smart brain again. By getting out there socialising and interacting with people, we also help others out too. Humans thrive on building relationships and communicating, and in doing so we can help each other build healthy happy brains.

Worksheets - Depression and the brain

TASK 1

Decreasing the intensity of depression

1A. Think of an event or time when your mood felt flat or depressed. Use your journal or a separate piece of paper to identify the following three things:

- What is the emotion you are feeling?
- What are your thoughts associated with this emotion? What are your needs?
- What is a possible solution to manage this emotion/s and thought/s?

Hint: The solution could be anything that makes you feel emotionally in control. For example, going for a walk, having a cup of tea, confronting the stressor or listening to music.

1B. Be assertive and say 'no' to certain activities and people. Remember to go at your pace not the pace of others. You do not need to give a response straight away.

Provide an example of a time when you were assertive or a time when being assertive would have helped the situation better.

1C. Identify when you are using negative self-talk and re-frame it. Choosing positive thoughts instead of negative ones, reminding yourself that depression is a temporary emotional state, and focus on taking one day at a time.

Try some of these examples:

I am so bad at maths, why try?	**CHANGE TO**	*e.g. I will do my best on this work and be proud that I gave it a go*
I feel so flat I am not going to the event	**CHANGE TO**	*e.g. I am not locked into anything I will go and leave when I want*
I think she/he hates me	**CHANGE TO**	
I will fail this exam anyway, so why study?	**CHANGE TO**	
My parents never support me	**CHANGE TO**	
I don't know anyone, I don't want to go	**CHANGE TO**	

TASK 2

Prioritise and structure your day so you feel emotionally in control. A sense of control allows us to connect better with people around us and maintain our motivation to keep going and make good choices. Use your wonderful journal and list a priority of tasks for today or tomorrow.

HINT: 6:30am-7:00am: Walk (focus on 10 things you can see, hear and feel to become mindful and emotionally present).

7:00am: shower and get dressed, before going to school write down four things to be grateful for, etc.

TASK 3

Awareness

Awareness is very important for managing our emotions. Being aware of what works is beneficial for managing and regulating your mood. Keeping a journal can be a helpful tool for self-monitoring. For example, writing down the event or trigger and the technique that worked for you. Remember a single technique may not always work, you need to have a few options. Below are a few options to consider and practice. Try them, to see if they work for you.

The progressive muscle relaxation technique

3A. Use this script to learn the progressive muscle relaxation exercise. You can begin at either the head or the toes - this script begins with the toes.

- Make sure you are in a relaxed position, but not in a bent position, sitting with your neck upright or lying flat.
- Close your eyes if you are comfortable doing so, and then allow your focus to rest entirely on the sensations of each muscle group.
- Now focus your attention on your toes. Tense your toes - curl them tight, tight, tight or imagine pushing your foot into the earth. Now release. Feel the warmth flood into them. Feel the energy and warmth suffuse those muscles. With each exhalation of breath, feel how warmth flows into the toes. (Repeat the tense, hold, and release three times before moving on to the next muscle group. It is amazing how much tension remains after just one or two tightenings).
- Now focus on your calves and shins. Tighten them by pointing your toes, and feel the stretch down your shin and the contraction in your calf. Then reverse by pulling your toe up and pushing the heel forward. Feel the stretch down your calf and the contraction in your shin. (Again, repeat the tense, hold, and release three times, and each time notice the warmth and energy that suffuses the muscles as tension is released).

- Now focus on your thighs, tightening them by using the muscles above the knees and using the buttocks as little as possible. (Repeat three times, noticing warmth and energy).
- Now focus on your buttocks. Tighten them by squeezing them together. (Repeat three times, noticing warmth and energy).
- Now focus on your back and abdomen. Tighten this area by imagining a string pulling your belly button toward your spine. (Repeat three times, noticing warmth and energy).
- Now focus on your arms. Tighten your forearm, wrist, and hand by clenching your fist. (Repeat three times, noticing warmth and energy).
- Now focus on your shoulders. Raise your shoulders up, hunching them. (Repeat three times, noticing warmth and energy).

Exercise

3B. Going for a brisk walk or run is helpful for; increasing the mood chemical, serotonin, reducing body tension, improving sleep, increasing feelings of wellbeing, increasing energy levels and reducing stress.

Meditation

3C. Guided meditation or self-directed meditation. There are many mobile apps to download for both iPhone and Android users. Here are a few examples of free ones:

- Relax Melodies
- Meditation Timer Pro
- Headspace
- Smiling Mind
- The Mindfulness App

Value system

3D. It is important at this stage to write in your journal what your values are. Some areas to think about are health, relationships and school. If you are not living your life in accordance with your value system this may affect your mood.

Summary

Managing depression and anxiety is about total self-care. Identifying which techniques work well for you and reinforcing them through repetition, you will develop automatic learned behaviours.

Sleep and the brain

Apart from breathing, good replenishing sleep is one of the most important things for human beings to be healthy. A healthy sleep cycle is made up of several stages, with two main states of sleep, the rapid eye movement (REM) phase (when you are likely to dream) and the non rapid eye movement phase (NREM), when we experience deep sleep.

Both phases are extremely important. To understand how they work, we will use this graph to track Steve's sleep cycle. From the first moment when Steve begins to fall asleep he goes through an NREM phase. This is split up into four distinct stages, as Steve eventually sinks into deep sleep.

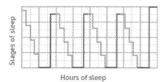

The next stage sees Steve start to dream in his first REM phase. This is when we are a lot closer to wakefulness and we are most likely to see experience sleepwalking or talking in our sleep.

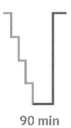

90 min

During an REM phase, a part of the brain called the hippocampus (which is the Greek word for sea-horse, because of its shape) processes all the information we have received during the day and feeds it into the smart

brain for long-term memory storage. This process is called hippocampal discharge.

After an REM phase, the brain waves once again sink back down into deep sleep for a while before moving into another REM or dream phase. It usually takes us around ninety minutes to progress through all four stages of NREM sleep and an REM phase. This makes up one cycle of sleep. There are usually four of these cycles in total within a healthy night's sleep.

It is then after the final stages of our last REM phase that we wake up. While we are sleeping, a very important process is taking place. During each REM phase, the brain chemical BDNF (brain-derived neurotrophic factor) is being produced. BDNF helps the brain to stay plastic or moldable. This means brain neurons can be joined together to form new pathways of communication.

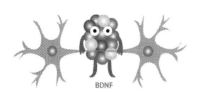

BDNF can also build new neurons. If the brain can't produce enough BDNF neurons during REM sleep phases it will eventually become deficient in this chemical. Without BDNF new neurons cannot be made and the existing ones become rigid.

Also the ability to connect (while the connection of neurons promote effective communication), particularly between the impulsive brain and smart brain, is compromised. If the brain is unable to create these pathways of communication the brain will not thrive, but merely survive.

In addition, the risk of developing neuron-degenerative disorders such as Alzheimer's disease or dementia, may increase. With such important processes taking place during both our REM and NREM phases of sleep, it is easy to see why good night's sleep is so vital for supporting the growth of and maintaining a healthy brain.

Now, you may wonder how much sleep do we actually need? On average we need eight hours. We may not get it all the time but we should aim for eight hours of good quality sleep, regularly. This will ensure our brains are producing enough BDNF, which will help them stay plastic and to develop new neurons at a rate that will keep our brains healthy and thriving.

Worksheets- Sleep and the brain

TASK 1

Revisiting the sleep states

1. What are the two main states of sleep?*

_____

_____

2. During what stage in sleep do we process all the information we have received during the day and transfer it into the smart brain for long term memory? What is this process called?

_____

_____

TASK 2

How do we know how many hours sleep we need?

In your journal let's determine how many hours of sleep you need for optimal functioning. Consider answering the following questions to estimate the natural length of your sleep cycle.

*   How many hours on average did you sleep as a child?
*   Before you started experiencing disrupted sleeping patterns, on average how many hours were you sleeping?
*   When you wake naturally (without an alarm) how many hours sleep have you completed?
*   How many hours sleep do you need to feel well rested and alert?
*   What rituals do you perform to signal to the brain that you are at the end of the day?

TASK 3

Identifying areas to improve sleep and health behaviours

Use your journal or the space provided below, to finish the statements and give you insight:

1. My sleep is disrupted when...
2. It feels like ....
3. It prevents ....
4. It results in..
5. It benefits me to...
6. To get my needs met I would..
7. I am prepared to..

TASK 4

Comfort and restful strategies

Things that provide comfort and security	Things that provide positive or negative effect on sleep	How can I improve them or stop them?	Strategy
e.g.	*e.g.*	*e.g*	*e.g.*
Eating something sweet as comfort before bed	*Negative - unable to fall asleep*	*Eating something low in sugar and well before bed time*	*Plan my meals and food*
Running after work	*Negative - speeds metabolism, causes arousa,*	*Run early morning instead*	*Schedule running days*

Answers: 1. The rapid eye movement phase or REM phase. This is when you are likely to dream and the non-rapid eye movement phase or NREM phase when we experience deep sleep. 2. During an REM phase. This process is called hippocampal discharge.

Reflection

1. How much did you know about sleep before you started this guide?
2. What did you discover about yourself as you worked through specific areas to improve your sleep?
3. Have you changed any ideas you used to have on your sleep management?
4. What would be your first goal you would like to set for yourself?

OCD and the brain

Obsessive compulsive disorder or OCD is a type of anxiety disorder where people experience either obsessive thought patterns, compulsive tendencies or in some cases both of these symptoms. OCD involves faulty communication between several parts of the brain leading to problems with initiation and completion of certain behaviours.

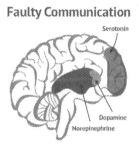

Faulty Communication

There are different theories about how OCD is develops. It may happen by observing others or there may be a genetic disposition, in which we might inherit an obsessive tendency. Another theory suggests that it may be related to a chemical imbalance in the brain, and this is the theory we will be exploring here.

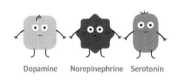

Dopamine   Norepinephrine   Serotonin

There are three main chemicals which when out of balance, may can cause unhelpful obsessive thought patterns. They are dopamine, norepinephrine (noradrenalin) serotonin. These are all neurotransmitters, which carry information from one part of the brain to another.

If they are out of balance, we may start to see a breakdown of communication and unhealthy thought loops start to develop in the impulsive brain. Let's take a closer look at these three brain chemicals.

Dopamine

Dopamine is produced in a section of the brain called the basal ganglia. Let us call it the 'motivation centre' of the brain. It gives us a sense of completion and accomplishment and lets us know we can move on to the next task.

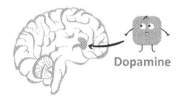

However, if we have a low level of dopamine we feel as so something is never quite finished until enough dopamine is released. We can see how this contributes to OCD, where people feel compelled to repeat an action or thought process much longer than it is necessary because, there isn't enough dopamine to trigger the feeling of completion.

Norepinephrine

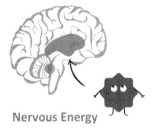

Norepinephrine is a brain chemical that activates our danger response and puts us on high alert. We could also think of it as the nervous energy chemical. While all OCDs sufferers show higher level of this nervous energy chemical, people exhibiting compulsive tendencies show much higher levels of it.

Serotonin

Serotonin is a brain chemical which regulates and maintains a healthy mood balance. We can think of it as a smart energy chemical. Our smart brains need adequate amount of this chemical because without it we lose the healthy communication between our smart brains and impulsive brains.

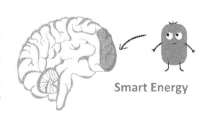

A key part of how communication starts to breakdown when someone experiences OCD is an unbalanced distribution of dopamine, the motivation chemical. The motivation centre is supposed to send dopamine to the hippocampus, the connection station of the brain that talks to the smart brain. It then sends information to the smart brain to provide us with the healthy sense of completion. But if there is too much of the nervous energy chemical in the brain (norepinephrine), large amounts of dopamine gets diverted there instead where its burned off in an effort to neutralise the nervous energy.

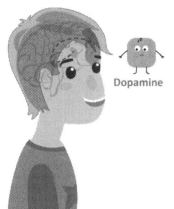

Dopamine

Due to this there is very little dopamine left for the hippocampus and smart brain, and it is this that promotes all those unhealthy brain-loops.

Experiencing OCD doesn't always mean experiencing both obsessive and compulsive tendencies. It is the special mix of these three main brain chemicals that determine which symptoms an OCD sufferer might experience.

Compulsive tendencies are repetitive behaviours where someone feels a compulsion to act on something without having any sense of reason about stopping. If these actions are repeated frequently enough over time, they become very strongly wired behaviours.

Here, Steve feels the compulsion to switch off the empty power sockets and doesn't feel comfortable until he is repeated this five times. He is experiencing; a low level of serotonin (or smart energy) so he can't reason properly, low levels of dopamine so he won't feel satisfied until his behavior has been repeated many times, very high levels of norepinephrine (or nervous energy) making him nervous and highly agitated, until he feels he's completed his task.

Obsessive tendencies on the other hand, refer to obsessive thought patterns, rather than actions. Steve has a fear of sharks which might be understandable in the context of swimming far out in the ocean. But if he is miles away and safe at home, and he is still dreading of a shark attack, this begins to form an obsessive thought pattern. Here there is a low level of serotonin so there is no reasoning, a low level of dopamine so he isn't satisfied to just let his thoughts rest, and moderate levels of norepinephrine making him anxious.

In order to beat OCD we have to develop new brain patterns, good chemical action, and to replace the harmful thought loops with healthier pathways of communication.

It is fine to have habits and routines that make us feel more comfortable and safe, but obsessing over things can actually turn a good habit into a bad one. Forming new habits will help increase those all-important dopamine levels and a healthy completion response will be restored once again in the brain.

Good patterns of sleep, nutrition and exercise and socialising with others will help to maintain healthy levels of brain chemicals and reinforce strong communication to the smart brain. Sometimes medication can help too, but only when you work with someone to build new brain pathways and develop healthy lifestyle habits. OCD is difficult to overcome, but we can change our brains to enjoy our lives much more.

Worksheets - Obsessional compulsive disorder (OCD) and the brain

TASK 1

1A. What are the three main chemicals that may cause unhelpful obsessive thought patterns (Hint: check the illustration).

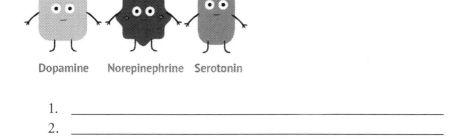

Dopamine   Norepinephrine   Serotonin

1. _____
2. _____
3. _____

1B. Dopamine is produced in the brain in an area called the basal ganglia. It gives us a sense of completion and accomplishment and lets us know we can move on to the next task. However, if we have a low level of dopamine, we feel as so something is never quite finished until enough dopamine is released. Then we sometimes feel compelled to repeat an action or thought process repeatedly or for much longer than is really required.

In your journal can you revisit an event/s where this may have had a negative impact, on some or all of the below categories. Write it in any format that allows you to express the sequence of the event (for example, dot point form or narrative).

- Personal growth and goals
- Work/school activities
- Social interactions and functioning
- Domestic role and functioning
- Significant relationships

TASK 2

2A. All OCD sufferers show higher levels of the nervous energy chemical norepinephrine. This nervous energy chemical has a significant impact on our patterns of behaviour, dynamics in relationships / social settings and negative impact on ourselves and/or others.

In your journal reflect on a time when you felt you had this heightened feeling of nervous energy that may have impacted all or some of those above categories. Again, write it in any format that allows you to express the sequence of the event (for example, dot point form or narrative).

Mindfulness with awareness

2B. Mindfulness is being aware of how you are thinking and feeling at any point in time. Think of this event and now close your eyes and breathe, noticing how your body feels (sitting in the chair / couch etc.), how the intake of air through your nose or mouth feels, how your heart beats and so on.

If it feels comfortable remain with your eyes closed, and now focus on what you can hear or maybe smell noticing things around you.

The purpose of this exercise is to show individuals with OCD that you can learn in a physical way that you can control what you notice about your world, whether internal or external. You are also in control of the pace and rhythm of your breathing. You will be then able to stop those repetitive negative thought loops, and feel more in control as you stay mindful of now rather than the future.

TASK 3

3A.* Serotonin regulates and maintains a healthy mood balance. Why do we need good levels of serotonin? Explain this in your own words:

_____

_____

_____

_____

_____

3B.* What are some ways to maintain and produce serotonin? Try to explain this:

_____

_____

_____

_____

_____

TASK 4

Below are two suggestion boxes to put your positive and constructive coping strategies into practice. You may wish to complete both boxes or select just one.

Obsessive thoughts controlled

Obsessive thoughts are:

When I have these thoughts, I will do the following things:

(for example, mindfulness activity, listen to music, speak to someone, etc.)

Compulsion/s	Do the compulsion/s 'feed' feelings of anxiety or control them?	How can I gradually reduce compulsion/s and control feelings of anxiety?
e.g. I need to check the locks on the front door or something bad may happen	*e.g. Yes, it increases if I don't check the lock properly*	*e.g. Have a worry time - setting a time limit for this process (the less time you spend on your worries the less anxiety you are likely to experience)* *Using relaxation or distraction techniques*

Reflection

1. What did you learn about yourself as you worked on this section?
2. What did you learn today that challenged you, empowered you or both?
3. As you reflect on the work you have done in this section, what do you feel you do well? What is the one thing you would like to improve upon?

Summary

In the last four sections the underlying message that you are learning to feel the way you think. There are four strategies to remember:

1. Thinking realistically
2. Recognising that your obsessional thoughts are only thoughts and your brain is sending false signals
3. Be mindful of what you are capable of doing right now
4. Focusing on what makes you feel confident, secure and positive

Remember that the brain is producing a signal that is false, and wanting you to repeat a task to 'make you feel good'. Ignore it, without giving it significance, and take control with mindfulness.

Answers: 3A. To have strong and healthy communication between our smart brain and impulsive brain. 3B. Good patterns of sleep, nutrition and exercise and socialising with others will help to maintain healthy levels of brain chemicals and reinforce strong communication to the smart brain.

Necessary ingredients to feel emotional control

1. Taking Responsibility

Whether the anxiety, depression, sleep disturbance or OCD is attributed to hereditary, trauma or ongoing stress in your life, you are ultimately responsible for either holding on to it, or being able to do something about it. Accepting responsibility for how you feel is the most empowering step you can take.

Taking responsibility means two things:

- You don't blame yourself for your difficulties, or anyone else. Is there any benefit blaming yourself for panic attacks, depression, sleeping disorders or obsessions and compulsions? Isn't it more supportive to say to yourself "I have done my best to manage my life up to now, with the knowledge and resources I have?"
- Taking responsibility to overcome the negative emotions you are experiencing, must be done in an enriched and supportive environment.

2. Motivation - Identifying Secondary Gains

To date, the motivation to 'stay in the condition' has consciously or unconsciously rewarded you for holding on to it. It may be feelings of familiarity, security or inability to trust yourself that change *can* happen, with the right support systems. If you find it difficult to sustain the positive changes or even initiate them, ask yourself these questions:

- "What benefit do I get staying this way?"
- "Do I deserve to feel happy and enjoy life?"

- "Is it really too much work to truly change?"
- "Can I go at my own pace and take small steps every day?"

3. Making a Commitment to Yourself

The initial commitment for change is usually strong. The actual test is being able to sustain the learned strategies and techniques over the long term. On a practical level, we learn new things like language, dancing, or any subject content by repetition. Repetition develops strong new neural pathways so that new learned behaviours can eventually occur automatically and naturally, without us needing to think about it.

4. Willingness to take risks

For any change to happen we need to take small risks. To reach for recovery we need to develop new ways of thinking, feeling and behaving. It may feel foreign and a little uncomfortable at first, but through repetition and practice it will become more familiar and safe. Having positive supportive people around you will also make taking risks that bit easier.

5. Defining your goals for long term happiness

Having a clear structure of the goals you are aiming for helps direct a clear path. Defining what your own recovery would look like, it is helpful to visualise it and maybe consider the following four questions:

- What are the key positive changes I would like to make in my life?
- What would a complete recovery from my condition look like?
- When I fully recover how will I think, feel and behave to myself and others?
- Once recovered, what new opportunities would I consider taking on?

This is another great opportunity to use your journal to write out a script of how your life would look and feel when you have fully recovered. This will increase your confidence about succeeding, because it will start to feel real when you use real parts of your life in the script. You may wish to also include pictures or photos.

References

Ainsworth, M. D., Blehar, M. C., Waters, E., & Wall, S. (1978). Patterns of attachment: A psychological study of the strange situation. Hillsdale, NJ: Lawrence Erlbaum Associates, Inc.

Allison, K. L., & Rossouw, P. J. (2013). The therapeutic alliance: Exploring the concept of "safety" from a neuropsychotherapeutic perspective. International Journal of Neuropsychotherapy, 1(1), 21-29. doi: 10.12744/ijnpt.2013.0021-0029.

Arden, J. B., & Linford, L. (2009). Brain-based therapy with adults: Evidence-based treatment for everyday practice. Hoboken, NJ: Wiley.

Badenoch, B. (2008). Being a brain-wise therapist: A practical guide to interpersonal neurobiology. New York, NY: W. W. Norton & Co.

Badenoch, B. (2011). The brain-savvy therapist's workbook. New York, NY: W. W. Norton & Co.

Baer, R. A., Smith, G. T., Hopkins, J., Krietemeyer, J., & Toney, L. (2006). Using self-report assessment methods to explore facets of mindfulness. Assessment, 13(1), 27-45.

Boden, J. M., Fergusson, D. M., & Horwood, L. J. (2008). Does adolescent self- esteem predict later life outcomes? A test of the causal role of self-esteem. Development and Psychopathology, 20, 319– 339.

Bowlby, J. (1973). Attachment and loss. Volume 1: Attachment. New York: Basic Books.

Bowlby, J. (1988). A secure base: parent-child attachment and healthy human development. New York: Basic Books.

Bowlby, J. (2008). Attachment: Volume One of the Attachment and Loss Trilogy: Attachment Vol 1 (Attachment & Loss) (Revised edition). Vintage Digital.

Cacioppo, J. T., Visser, P. S., & Pickett, C. L. (2006). Social neuroscience: People thinking about people. Cambridge, Massachusetts: Massachusetts Institute of Technology.

Cozolino, L. (2014). The neuroscience of human relationships: Attachment and the developing social brain. New York, NY: W. W. Norton & Co.

Dahlitz, M. J. (2013). Klaus Grawe. The Neuropsychotherapist, 2, 128-129.

Dahlitz, M. J., & Rossouw, P. J. (2014). The consistency-theoretical model of mental functioning: Towards a refined perspective. In Rossouw, P. J. (Ed.), Neuropsychotherapy: Theoretical underpinnings and clinical applications. Brisbane, Qld: Mediros Pty Ltd.

Ecker, B. (2015). Memory reconsolidation understood and misunderstood. International Journal of Neuropsychotherapy, 3(1), 2–46. doi: 10.12744/ijnpt.2015.0002-0046

Elliot, A. J. (2006). The hierarchal model of approach-avoidance motivation. Motivation and Emotion, 30, 111-116.

Elliot, A. J. (2008). Handbook of approach and avoidance motivation. New York, NY: Psychology Press.

Feingberg, T. E., & Keenan, J. P. (2005). Where in the brain is the self? Consciousness and Cognition, 14, 661-678.

Flückiger, C., Caspar, F., Grosse Holtforth, M., & Willutzki, U. (2009). Working with patients' strengths: A microprocess approach. Psychotherapy Research, 19(2), 213-223.

Flückiger, C., Wüsten, G., Zinbarg, R. E., & Wampold, B. E. (2009). Resource activation: Using clients' own strengths in psychotherapy and counseling. Cambridge, MA: Hogrefe & Huber Publishers.

Freud, S. (1959). Beyond the pleasure principle. New York, NY: W. W. Norton & Co. (Original work published in 1920)

Freud, S. (1966). Project for a scientific psychology. In J. Strachey (Ed. & Trans.), The standard edition of the complete psychological works of Sigmund Freud (Vol. 1. Pp. 281-392). London: Hogarth Press. (Original work published 1895)

Gassmann, D., & Grawe, K. (2006). General change mechanisms: The relation between problem activation and resource activation in successful and unsuccessful therapeutic interactions. Clinical Psychology and Psychotherapy, 13(1), 1-11.

Grawe, K. (2004). Psychological therapy. Toronto: Hogrefe & Huber.

Grawe, K. (2007). Neuropsychotherapy: How the neurosciences inform effective psychotherapy. New York, NY: Psychology Press.

Hubel, D., & Wiesel, T. (2012). Neuron. The Journal of Physiology, 75(2), 182-184.

Kandel, E. R. (1998). A new intellectual framework for psychiatry. American Journal of Psychiatry, 155, 457–469.

Kandel, E. R., Schwartz, J. H., Jessell, T. M., Siegelbaum, S.A., & Hudspeth, A. J. (Eds.) (2013). Principles of Neural Science, 5th ed. New York, NY: McGraw-Hill.

Keleman, S. (2012). Slow Attending: The Art of Forming Intimacy. Retrieved September 3, 2014, from http://www.neuropsychotherapist.com/slow-attending-article doi: 10.12744/tnpt.06.01.2013.01

Lupien, S. J., McEwen, B. S., Gunnar, M. R., & Heim, C. (2009). Effects of stress throughout the lifespan on the brain, behaviour and cognition. Nature Reviews Neuroscience, 10, 434-445. doi:10.1038/nrn2639

MacLean, P. D. (1990). The triune brain in evolution: Role in paleocerebral functions. New York: Plenum Press.

McGilchrist, L (2009). The Master and His Emissary: The Divided Brain and the Making of the Western World. London :Yale university Press

Montgomery, A. (2013). Neurobiology essentials for clinicians: What every therapist needs to know. New York, NY: W. W. Norton & Co.

Rossouw, P. J. (2011). The triune brain: Implications for neuropsychotherapy. Neuropsychotherapy, 5, 2-3.

Rossouw, P. J. (2012a). The Neurobiological Markers of Childhood Trauma: Implications for therapeutic interventions. Retrieved 08/27/2014 from http://www.neuropsychotherapist.com/childhood-trauma

Rossouw, P. J. (2012b). Effective client focused interventions: The top-down and bottom-up discourse. Neuropsychotherapy News, 11, 2–4. Retrieved from http://mediros.com.au/wp-content/uploads/2012/11/NPTIG-Newsletter-11.pdf

Rossouw, P. J. (2012c). Neuroscience, learning and memory: From sea slugs to mental health. Neuropsychotherapy News, 13, 2–6. Retrieved from http://mediros.com.au/wp-content/uploads/2012/11/NPTIG-Newsletter-13.pdf

Rossouw, P. J. (2013). The neurobiological underpinnings of the mental health renaissance. The Neuropsychotherapist, 1, 14–21. doi: http://dx.doi.org/10.12744/tnpt(1)014-021

Rossouw, P. J. (2013b). The end of the medical model: Recent findings in neuroscience regarding antidepressant medication and the implications for neuropsychotherapy. The Neuropsychotherapist.

Retrieved from http://www.neuropsychotherapist.com/the-end-of-the-medical-model/

Rossouw, P. J. (2014) (Ed.). Neuropsychotherapy: Theoretical underpinnings and clinical applications. Brisbane, Qld: Mediros Pty Ltd.

Sacktor, T. C. (2008). PKMzeta, LTP maintenance, and the dynamic molecular biology of memory storage. Progress in Brain Research, 169, 27-40.

Sacktor, T. C. (2010). How does PKMzeta maintain long-term memory? Nature Reviews Neuroscience, 12(1), 9-15

Scaer, R. C., (2005). The trauma spectrum: Hidden wounds and human resiliency. New York, NY: W. W. Norton & Co.

Schore, A. N. (1994). Affect regulation and the origin of the self. Mahwah, NJ: Erlbaum.

Schore, A. N. (2003a). Affect regulation and the repair of the self. New York, NY: W. W. Norton & Co.

Schore, A. N. (2003b). Affect dysregulation and disorders of the self. New York, NY: W. W. Norton & Co.

Schore, A. N. (2003c). Early relational trauma, disorganised attachment, and the development of a predisposition to violence. In Solomon, M. F., & Siegel, D. J. (Eds.), Healing Trauma: Attachment, mind, body, and brain (pp. 107-167). New York, NY: W. W. Norton & Co.

Schore, A. N. (2012). The science of the art of psychotherapy. New York, NY: W. W. Norton & Co.

Schore, A. N. (2014). The right brain is dominant in psychotherapy. Psychotherapy, 51(3), 388-397. Doi: 10.1037/a0037083.

Schore, J. R., & Schore, A. N. (2008). Modern attachment theory: The central role of affect regulation in development and treatment. Clinical Social Work Journal, 36, 9-20.

Siegel, D. J. (1999). The developing mind: How relationships and the brain interact to shape who we are. New York, NY: Guilford Press.

Siegel, D. J. (2007). The mindful brain: Reflections and attunement in the cultivation of well-being. New York, NY: W. W. Norton & Co.

Siegel, D. J. (2010). The mindful therapist: A clinician's guide to mindsight and neural integration. New York, NY: Norton.

Siegel, D. J. (2012). The developing mind: How relationships and the brain interact to shape who we are. (Second Ed.). New York, NY: Guilford Press.

Smith, E. C. and Grawe, K. (2003), What makes psychotherapy sessions productive? a new approach to bridging the gap between process research and practice. Clinical Psychology & Psychotherapy, 10, 275–285. doi: 10.1002/cpp.377

The Neuropsychotherapy Institute (Producer). (2014a). Genes, Neurons & Glia: The Wonder of the Social Brain [Online Video]. Retrieved from

http://neuropsychotherapist.com/institute/genes-neurons-glia/

The Neuropsychotherapy Institute (Producer). (2014b). Key Neurochemicals [Online Video]. Retrieved from http://neuropsychotherapist.com/institute/c07-key-neurochemicals/

The Neuropsychotherapy Institute (Producer). (2014c). The Triune Brain: Implications for Neuropsychotherapy [Online Video]. Retrieved from http://neuropsychotherapist.com/institute/the-triune-brain/

The Neuropsychotherapy Institute (Producer). (2014d). Cortical Blood Flow & Neural Connectivity [Online Video]. Retrieved from http://neuro psychotherapist.com/institute/ cortical-blood-flow-neural-connectivity/

Verkhratsky, A., & Butt, A. (2007). Glial neurobiology: A textbook. Chichester, West Sussex: John Wiley & Sons Ltd.

Zhao, X., Li, Y., Peng, T., Seese, R. R., & Wang, Z. (2011). Stress impairs consolidation of recognition memory after blocking drug memory reconsolidation. Neuroscience Letters, 501(1), 50-54.

Printed in the United States
By Bookmasters